The Entertainment Ministry

PRESENTS

CHARLES DICKENS' *A Christmas Carol Bible Study*

study guide

WRITER: *Stephen Skelton*

CREATIVE: *Jim Howell, Judy Northcutt Gaertner*

A Christmas Carol BIBLE STUDY
PUBLISHED BY *The Entertainment Ministry, LLC*

Printed Materials © 2006 by The Entertainment Ministry, LLC

Scripture quotations taken from the HOLY BIBLE, NEW INTERNATIONAL VERSION. Copyright © 1973, 1978, 1984 by International Bible Society. Used by permission of Zondervan Publishing House.

Written materials are creation of author and not endorsed by actors, producers, creators or copyright holders of film. Images from public domain film.

Printed in the United States of America

ISBN 0-9765142-9-X

To order or receive more information: *TOLL FREE* **1-877-GOD-IN TV** *(1-877-463-4688)*
www.EntertainmentMinistry.com

For speaking engagements with author Stephen Skelton: **1-615-263-4143 x:234**

INTRODUCTION

Biblical Basis

To illustrate a principle, Jesus often used a parable—an earthly story with a heavenly meaning. Parables allow listeners to recognize real-life events as relevant examples of spiritual truth. In this way, these short stories link what we already know to what we should believe. Those that resist only hear a trivial story, while those that look past the surface find meaning.

Scriptural Precedents

In the parables, Christians have a precedent for utilizing stories for testimony. Interestingly, whether Good Samaritan (Lk 10:30-37), Lost Son (Lk 15:11-32) or Unforgiving Servant (Mt 18:23-35), parable characters did not proclaim the Good News. Indeed, our soap operas today feature similar dramatic narratives. Yet Christ used these secular stories to convey Gospel Truth.

In another direct example, Paul used references from the popular culture to communicate a spiritual message when he cited certain Pagan poets (Ac 17:28) and named the unknown god (Ac 17:22-24). In fact, when Paul said, "'Bad company corrupts good character'" (1 Co 15:33), he was quoting a line of dialogue from a theater play (Greek comedy *Thais* written by Menader).

Modern Parables

Because the Bible is the most influential book in the world, modern writers borrow from it more often than we might think, whether they realize it or not. One fundamental way to use popular entertainment to engage a Christian worldview is to evaluate the story events from a Scriptural perspective. Even a casual conversation about a TV show can afford an opportunity to witness.

To identify God's purposes, first we should examine the overall program in terms of Biblical themes. Next, we should focus that lens on story lines, characters and names. Lastly, we need to use that information as a testimonial tool: mention what a character said about the Lord; uncover the Biblical meaning behind the names; then share how you were saved.

A Christmas Carol Bible Study

Already, many of you have used these studies to successfully reach adults, young people, non-church members—even to refresh the world-weary souls of longtime believers. For those new to these studies, ask yourself… Do you want to engage and energize your class… Do you want to bring Jesus to searchers "where they are"… Do you want to model the powerful parable approach of Christ…
Then you can use *A Christmas Carol Bible Study*.

Blessings,

Stephen Skelton
The Entertainment Ministry

ABOUT THE AUTHOR

Stephen Skelton, founder of The Entertainment Ministry,
serves as host for *A Christmas Carol Bible Study*. Previously, he has served
as a writer-producer with Dick Clark Productions. In addition, he is the author of
The Gospel According to the World's Greatest Superhero. As a Christian in the
entertainment industry, Stephen seeks to identify God's purposes in popular entertainment.
Stephen lives in Nashville with his wife and children.

ABOUT THE ENTERTAINMENT MINISTRY

At The Entertainment Ministry, we believe many stories that transcend social,
racial and cultural barriers today do so because they contain spiritual truth
for which all people have a God-given hunger. Accordingly, the ministry promotes
a grassroots approach to using popular entertainment to engage a Christian worldview.
To that end, we hope these Bible studies not only provide a time of good fellowship,
but also continue to equip the church with ways to reach the world beyond.

TABLE OF CONTENTS

THE STORY

This section, *"Scrooge,"* introduces the selfish miser himself—
a man so self-centered, not even Christmas Eve can put him in a
giving mood. When clerk Bob Cratchit tries to stoke the office fire,
Scrooge denies the cold man a piece of coal. And when nephew
Fred invites him to Christmas dinner, Scrooge rudely refuses to
fellowship with his own family. Only later that night does Scrooge
find himself at a loss, when his deceased partner Jacob Marley
appears to accuse his selfish soul.

THE MORAL OF THE STORY

*This lesson, **"Bab Humbug!,"** highlights the Biblical principle
of Selfishness. The study examines how our selfishness is
really our attempt to control our own destiny, rather than
allow God to lead us. The lesson also addresses how, in
selfishly focusing on yourself, you create a self-imposed
prison—from which you cannot please yourself enough to free
yourself. The point of this study is that selfish people actually
cheat themselves out of the greatest possession they could
ever have: eternal life with God.*

CHARLES DICKENS' A

Christmas Carol

Bible Study

lesson 1

SECTION TITLE: **"Scrooge"**

LESSON TITLE: **"Bah Humbug!"**

BIBLICAL THEME: **Selfishness**

LESSON ONE
"Bah Humbug!"

<u>Unit Overview</u>

Parable

The Christ of Christmas...

> MARK 8:36
> *"What good is it for a man to gain the whole world, yet forfeit his soul?"* (NIV)

Reflection

From Humbug to Humble...

> LUKE 12:15
> *Then he said to them, "Watch out! Be on your guard against all kinds of greed; a man's life does not consist in the abundance of his possessions."* (NIV)

Action

God Bless Us Every One...

> PHILIPPIANS 2:3
> *Do nothing out of selfish ambition or vain conceit, but in humility consider others better than yourselves.* (NIV)

Selfishness

> MARK 8:36
>
> *"What good is it for a man to gain the whole world, yet forfeit his soul?"* (NIV)

If it wasn't for acting selfish, some of us wouldn't know how to act. After all, if we don't serve ourselves, how else will we get what we want before someone else gets it? However, we should be mindful of what we are giving up when we act this way. Ironically, in our selfish efforts to gain material things, we don't think twice about trading our eternal souls. Instead, we should be willing to give our very lives for the sake of Christ. Amazingly, in doing this, we will gain the satisfaction and security that we so desperately seek.

Parable

The Christ of Christmas…

In his selfishness, Scrooge was trapped by himself. Unable to please himself enough to free himself, he was mired in misery. Unfortunately, his selfishness made others miserable as well. Poor Bob Cratchit suffered by Scrooge's stinginess. And nephew Fred suffered by Scrooge's coldness. Of course, in cutting himself off from their kindness, Scrooge suffered from his own selfishness the most. Briefly, described how each dealt with selfishness.

As a book written during a time of decline in Christmas traditions, amazingly, *A Christmas Carol* actually helped to revive the celebration of Christmas around the world.

Scrooge: _____

Bob: _____

Fred: _____

When have you been selfish? What have you sacrificed for your selfishness?

_____

_____

_____

Selfishness is deceptive—especially to the selfish person. Although we seem to be looking out for number one, in fact we are blinded to how we are hurting ourselves. When we focus solely on ourselves and no others, we each create a self-imposed prison—in which we are unloving, unloved and unhappy. **God's way offers the glorious opposite of this (Ps 119:36).** *Consider how many ways Scrooge was selfish.*

How was Scrooge selfish—financially, emotionally, spiritually?
How did he show each side?

_____

_____

_____

We draw selfishness from the devil. And his type of inspiration is nothing to brag about. As with all sin, when we are selfish, while we may think we are being smart, we are only making fools of ourselves. **True wisdom reveals that bitter envy and selfish ambition damage everyone involved (Jas 3:14-15).** *Think about how Scrooge reacted to Bob and Fred's generosity.*

> Psalm 119:36
> Turn my heart toward your statutes and not toward selfish gain.

> James 3:14-15
> But if you harbor bitter envy and selfish ambition in your hearts, do not boast about it or deny the truth. 15) Such "wisdom" does not come down from heaven but is earthly, unspiritual, of the devil.

In Charles Dickens' time, a "carol" was known as a song of joy celebrating the birth of Christ.

How was Bob generous? How did
Scrooge exploit his generosity? Why?

_____

_____

_____

_____

How was nephew Fred generous?
How did Scrooge mock his generosity? Why?

_____

_____

_____

Selfish people get what they deserve, not necessarily what they want. For example, few selfish people would wish themselves poorer. Yet ultimately, poorer is what they become as they lose close connection with friends and loved ones. **By contrast, generous people can get more than they give as they receive both the satisfaction of being a service and the kindness of those they have helped (Pr 11:17).**

How was Scrooge made poor by his selfishness?
How was Bob made rich by his generosity?

_____

_____

_____

Proverbs 11:17
A kind man benefits himself, but a cruel man brings trouble on himself.

A Christmas Carol was pirated viciously. In London, it was first copied into stage plays. Next, it was reprinted in other books. In America, it was reprinted for pamphlets, newspapers and books.

Reflection

From Humbug to Humble…

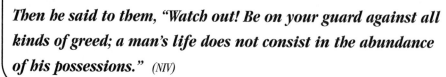

LUKE 12:15

***Then he said to them, "Watch out! Be on your guard against all
kinds of greed; a man's life does not consist in the abundance
of his possessions."*** (NIV)

*A sure sign of selfishness is greed. When it comes to material things, too
many of us mistake the quantity in our lives for the quality of our lives—
to our misery. **Even worse, in our intense focus on this life, we fail to
prepare for the next (Lk 12:20-21).** Indeed, your selfishness is really your
attempt to control your own destiny, rather than allow God to lead you.
**Contradictorily, in being so selfish, you actually cheat yourself
out of the greatest possession you could ever have: eternal life
(Ro 2:7-8).** Instead, you should think beyond your selfish goals to the
goodwill goal of helping others—and receiving heaven thereafter.*

Like Bob, have you seen a "Scrooge"
suffer from his own selfishness?
Give an example.

_____

_____

_____

Like Bob, have you suffered because
of the selfishness of someone else?
Give an example.

The character of
Bob Cratchit shared
some characteristics
with Charles Dickens'
father, John Dickens,
who was also a clerk
with a large family.

_____

_____

_____

*Fred was the selfless opposite of selfish Scrooge. Likewise, for us, sinful behavior such as bitterness, slander and malice—while they may be common to others—have no place in the Christian's life. These actions grieve the Holy Spirit that God placed inside of you to insure your redemption. **Instead, you should act in love toward others just as God has acted in love toward you (Eph 4:30-32).***

Like Fred, have you reached out to someone that was selfish toward you? Give an example.

_____

_____

_____

_____

*In his selfishness, Scrooge kept even himself from others. **In doing the same, any man defies sound judgment because he offends his fellow men and angers God (Pr 18:1).** Then that man becomes truly alone, unable to either give or receive help. In this, rather than securing your safety, you make yourself more vulnerable by turning away those that would support you during difficult times.*

Like Scrooge, has selfishness separated you from others in some way? Give an example.

_____

_____

_____

Ephesians 4:30-32
And do not grieve the Holy Spirit…
31) Get rid of all bitterness…and slander, along with every form of malice. 32) Be kind and compassionate to one another, forgiving each other, just as in Christ God forgave you.

Proverbs 18:1
An unfriendly man pursues selfish ends; he defies all sound judgment.

There were six children in young Charles Dickens' family—the same number of children as in Bob Cratchit's family.

Action

God Bless Us Every One…

> PHILLIPIANS 2:3
> *Do nothing out of selfish ambition or vain conceit, but in humility consider others better than yourselves.* (NIV)

Selfishness gives you a false view of yourself and others. This is one reason why you should never do anything out of selfishness. Because of its distorted view, selfishness destroys relationships as you try to serve yourself first. By contrast, humility builds relationships as it provides you with a true perspective of yourself in relation to others. With humility, you seek to meet the needs of others before your own. In short, when you act in humility, you act like Christ; when you act in selfishness, you act like Satan. **Like the devil, those with selfish motives will not inherit heaven (Eph 5:5). Instead, submit to others out of reverence for Christ (Eph 5:21).**

Why should you not be selfish?

_____

_____

_____

_____

_____

How can you stop being selfish?

_____

_____

_____

_____

_____

How do generous people receive
more than selfish people?

_____

_____

_____

_____

_____

I will live with less selfishness and more generosity by:

❏ Helping another person before myself when waiting in a line.

❏ Giving in some way—even when it is not convenient.

Specific: _____

_____

_____

_____

_____

In the *Carol* book,
Scrooge disapproves
of his nephew's
marrying because he
thought his nephew
did not have enough
money to support a
family, underscoring
Scrooge's emphasis
on money over love.

THE STORY

This section, *"Marley and the Ghost of Christmas Past,"* sees Scrooge regret the mistakes of his past—even as he learns that they will haunt his future. First, the ghost of Jacob Marley warns Scrooge that the sins of this life are punished in the next, as each of his misdeeds forges a link in a chain he will wear for eternity. Then, the Ghost of Christmas Past takes Scrooge back to the pivotal time when he first chose the love of money over a life of love—a tragic day, in a past of regret.

THE MORAL OF THE STORY

This lesson, "A Past of Regret," highlights the Biblical principle of Regret. The notes focus on how most of us will regret our sins twice—first in this life and later in the next. The study also addresses how we feel regret when our conscience says we have chosen to do what was wrong, even though we knew inside what was right. The goal of this lesson is to make clear that God can forgive what you regret—and the guilt you feel will be relieved as the reason for your regret is washed away.

CHARLES DICKENS' *A Christmas Carol Bible Study*

lesson 2

SECTION TITLE: **"Marley and the Ghost of Christmas Past"**

LESSON TITLE: **"A Past of Regret"**

BIBLICAL THEME: **Regret**

LESSON TWO
"A Past of Regret"

Unit Overview
Parable
The Christ of Christmas...

ECCLESIASTES 3:15
Whatever is has already been, and what will be has been before; and God will call the past to account. (NIV)

Reflection
From Humbug to Humble…

PSALM 51:17
The sacrifices of God are a broken spirit; a broken and contrite heart, O God, you will not despise. (NIV)

Action
God Bless Us Every One…

HEBREWS 10:22
let us draw near to God with a sincere heart in full assurance of faith, having our hearts sprinkled to cleanse us from a guilty conscience... (NIV)

Regret

> **ECCLESIASTES 3:15**
> *Whatever is has already been, and what will be has been before; and God will call the past to account.* (NIV)

Most of us will regret our sins twice—first in this life and later in the next. Although our punishment may not be immediate, God does not forget our wrongful actions, but will ask us to answer for them at his appointed time. In the meanwhile, regret can have a positive effect in that sincere sorrow over our past sins can spur us to improve ourselves morally. While it is easy to regret the sins that have hurt us, it is much harder to regret those sins we have benefited from, even though we should. Rather than ignoring a regret, use it to change your life for the better.

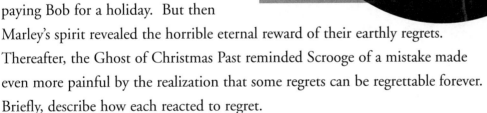

Parable

The Christ of Christmas…

Here, Scrooge learned what to truly regret—and why. Earlier, he regretted most the nuisance of his nephew's dinner invitation and the burden of paying Bob for a holiday. But then Marley's spirit revealed the horrible eternal reward of their earthly regrets. Thereafter, the Ghost of Christmas Past reminded Scrooge of a mistake made even more painful by the realization that some regrets can be regrettable forever. Briefly, describe how each reacted to regret.

Scrooge: _____

Marley: _____

Ghost: _____

Belle: _____

In the *Carol* book, Marley bemoans, "Why did I walk through crowds of fellow-beings with my eyes turned down, and never raise them to that blessed Star which led the Wise Men to a poor abode?"

What do you regret?

What will you change about your actions based on your regrets?

_____

_____

_____

Rarely is a regret only a thing of the past. That is, we may regret some mistakes in both the past and the future. In fact, our present may not be free from regret either, if we continue to make the same mistakes over and over. All of this is the punishment for foolishness. **The solution is an understanding of how God wants us to be (Pr 16:22).** *Consider Marley and his regrets.*

What did Marley regret from his past?

What did he regret for his future?

How were they linked?

_____

_____

_____

_____

How did Marley use his regret to benefit Scrooge?

Why did he warn Scrooge of judgment?

_____

_____

_____

God wants us to regret. And then he wants us to change for the better (2 Co 7:9). *As a guide on how to deal with regret—as well as how not to—two examples emerge from those who were closest to Christ. Both Peter and Judas felt regret after each disowned Jesus. However, whereas Peter used his regret to grow, Judas killed himself. Think about how Scrooge handled regret.*

What did Scrooge regret? How did facing his regret actually have a beneficial effect on him?

_____

_____

_____

_____

_____

Regret must be put into action. If we do nothing, we will stagnate spiritually and eventually suffer eternal death. ***Instead, we must "put to death the misdeeds of the body," meaning we must consider the appeal of sin as dead to us—and live accordingly (Ro 8:13).*** *In doing so, we will still sin and feel regret, but that regret is now a constant reminder to continue to act out our faith.*

What did Belle regret? What did she do about it? How hard was it to do the right thing?

_____

_____

_____

_____

Dickens had his own "Belle," of whom he wrote to a friend, "A sense comes always crushing on me now...as of one happiness I have missed in life, and one friend and companion I have never made..."

Reflection

From Humbug to Humble…

> **PSALM 51:17**
> *The sacrifices of God are a broken spirit; a broken and contrite heart, O God, you will not despise.* (NIV)

Regret reflects a longing to be right with God. God favors a contrite heart because it reveals a spirit broken over sorrow for sin. **This is the work of the Holy Spirit—to bring regret as he convicts you of your guilt (Jn 16:8).** *In doing so, the Holy Spirit affirms God's moral standards, which each one of you has written on your hearts.* **When you feel regret, it is your conscience saying you have chosen to do what was wrong, even though you knew inside what was right (Ro 2:14-15).** *Put simply then, what is written on your heart is God's law; the witness to how well you obey the law is your conscience; and the feeling you have at breaking the law is regret.*

Like Scrooge, have unresolved regrets created a broken spirit in you?

Give an example.

_____

_____

_____

Like Marley, have past regrets compelled you to follow the law on your heart? Give an example.

_____

_____

Belle made her regret beget a positive future. When we feel something is morally wrong, we should address the problem immediately. **With a clear conscience, you can eagerly look forward to the time of resurrection and judgment (Acts 24:15-16).** *To keep your conscience clean, do the right thing—and when you don't, confess your sins.*

Like Belle, have you avoided future regrets by addressing present regrets immediately? Give an example.

_____

_____

_____

_____

_____

Belle benefited more than just herself when she addressed her regret— as her family affirmed. Similarly, when you walk out your faith, others may receive a blessing. This happens when you add to your faith actions based on values such as goodness, godliness, brotherly kindness and love. **As a Christian, you can feel the power to do this when you remember your past sins have been forgiven so those regrets have no hold over you (2 Pe 1:5, 7, 9).**

Like Belle's husband, have you benefited by someone addressing their regrets? Give an example.

_____

_____

_____

Of the poor, Dickens wrote, "Heaven was made for them as well as for the rich, and God makes no difference between those who wear good clothes and those who go barefoot and in rags."

Action
God Bless Us Every One…

> HEBREWS 10:22
> ***let us draw near to God with a sincere heart in full assurance of faith, having our hearts sprinkled to cleanse us from a guilty conscience…*** *(NIV)*

God can forgive what you regret. Because you have access to God through Christ, you can ask him to forgive your sins. If you do so with a sincere heart, the guilt you feel will be washed away as the reason for your regret is forgiven. **When you have a guilty conscience, you will either repent or suffer because you refuse to repent (Pr 28:16, 18).** *Thus, if you soothe your troubled conscience by downplaying your sin, you are actually doing yourself a dangerous disservice.*

Guilt is a natural consequence of sin— and the more regret you feel the more you realize your need to repent (Jer 2:19). *God alone can cleanse your heart of guilt. And he is always waiting to relieve your regret.*

Why do you feel regret?

_____

_____

_____

_____

What should you regret?

_____

_____

_____

_____

What can God do about your regrets?

_____

_____

_____

_____

_____

_____

_____

I will live with regret in the right way by:

❏ Using my guilt as a spur to correct a moral wrong.

❏ Using my guilt as a signal to confess my sin to God.

Specific: _____

_____

_____

_____

_____

As a boy, Dickens loved a small collection of books that belonged to his father. Later in life, Charles fell into debt and, regretfully, had to pawn away these precious items.

THE STORY

This section, *"Ghost of Christmas Present,"* brings Scrooge to repentance as the cynic sees how Christmas should be kept. On Christmas day, the Cratchits prove that although they are poor in finances, more importantly, they are rich in family. And Scrooge is amazed at how well they love, despite how badly he treats their father Bob. In the end, Scrooge is both touched and shamed by the youngest member, Tiny Tim, who toasts to Scrooge's health even as his own fails him.

THE MORAL OF THE STORY

This lesson, "A Present Repentance," highlights the Biblical principle of Repentance. The notes look at how God provides "godly sorrow," which is sorrow that brings us to repentance. The study also explains how God patiently postpones the day of judgment to give us time to repent. The core message here is that, when we are repentant, we show God that we know we have sinned, we confess our sins to him and we acknowledge we need his power to continue to repent.

CHARLES DICKENS' *A Christmas Carol Bible Study*

lesson 3

SECTION TITLE: **"Ghost of Christmas Present"**

LESSON TITLE: **"A Present Repentance"**

BIBLICAL THEME: **Repentance**

LESSON THREE

"A Present Repentance"

Unit Overview

Parable

The Christ of Christmas...

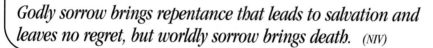

2 CORINTHIANS 7:10

Godly sorrow brings repentance that leads to salvation and leaves no regret, but worldly sorrow brings death. (NIV)

Reflection

From Humbug to Humble...

ROMANS 2:5
But because of your stubbornness and your unrepentant heart, you are storing up wrath against yourself for the day of God's wrath, when his righteous judgment will be revealed. (NIV)

Action

God Bless Us Every One...

1 JOHN 1:9-10
If we confess our sins, he is faithful and just and will forgive us our sins and purify us from all unrighteousness. If we claim we have not sinned, we make him out to be a liar and his word has no place in our lives. (NIV)

Repentance

2 CORINTHIANS 7:10
Godly sorrow brings repentance that leads to salvation and leaves no regret, but worldly sorrow brings death. (NIV)

Repentance means admitting we were wrong—that's why we don't like to repent. When confronted with our sins, too often we respond by becoming prideful and defensive. To help us, God provides "godly sorrow," which is sorrow that brings us to repent of our sin. By contrast, "worldly sorrow" is sorrow over worldly punishment, such as getting caught in a sin. Whereas godly sorrow motivates us to stop sinning, worldly sorrow only motivates us to stop getting caught. Thus, godly sorrow leads to eternal life, while worldly sorrow ends in eternal death.

Parable

The Christ of Christmas...

When the Ghost of Christmas Present transported Scrooge to the Cratchits, Scrooge repented of his cynical ideas about Christmas. First, Bob and Tiny Tim happily attended church. Next, the Cratchit family feasted on love as much as food. Finally, Bob sincerely toasted the health of his harsh employer. And who would have believed that a frail boy on a crutch could have broken the hard heart of Ebenezer Scrooge? Briefly, tell how each person interacted with repentance.

Scrooge: _____

Ghost: _____

Bob: _____

Tiny Tim: _____

The name "Cratchit" likely comes from "cratch," an old English word for crèche, the manger in which the infant Jesus laid.

What have you repented of?

What brought you to repentance?

_____

_____

_____

Repentance comes after regret for those who learn from their mistakes. However, it is impossible to repent from a mistake you do not admit you made. **Covering over sins may be a natural human reaction, but it offers us no real benefit because it dooms us to repeat our mistakes. Rather than repeat, we should repent (Pr 28:13).** *Consider how Scrooge became repentant.*

Why was Scrooge more repentant during this visit?
How had his regret prepared him for repentance?

_____

_____

_____

How does repentance become heartfelt? Often, there is a difference between hearing about a thing and experiencing that thing firsthand. **Job learned this about God when his eyes saw what his ears had only heard about (Job 42:5-6).** *To make our repentance heartfelt, we might need to examine the effects of our actions. Think about how the Cratchits affected the repentance of Scrooge.*

Scrooge pays Bob
fifteen shillings a
week—which was the
amount Dickens was
paid as an office boy.
While fine for a
teenage boy, the pay
was much too little
for a family
man like Bob.

How did the Cratchits make repentance more personal for Scrooge?
Why was this connection important?

_____

_____

_____

How did Tiny Tim compel Scrooge
toward repentance? How was Tim
both less fortunate and more giving?

_____

_____

_____

_____

_____

Repentance should bear fruit. This is a way of saying that God expects more from our repentance than words and rituals. **When we sin, we should repent and then we should do good deeds (Mt 3:8).** *For Christians, the alternative is to call ourselves God's people and then do nothing for either God or people. If we bear fruit, we are useful; we are useless if we are barren.*

Matthew 3:8
"Produce fruit in keeping
with repentance."

How did the Ghost hint that Scrooge could change the fate of Tiny Tim?
How did this raise the stakes on Scrooge's repentance?

_____

_____

_____

The description of
Dickens as a child—
"a very little and
very sickly boy,
subject to attacks of
violent spasm which
disabled him from any
active exertion"—
would fit Tiny Tim.

Reflection

From Humbug to Humble...

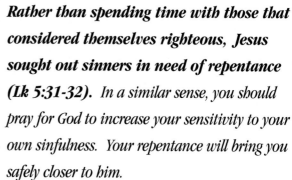

ROMANS 2:5
But because of your stubbornness and your unrepentant heart, you are storing up wrath against yourself for the day of God's wrath, when his righteous judgment will be revealed. (NIV)

Repentance releases the wrath of God that is building up against our sin. When we have unrepentant hearts, God's anger stores up for the day of judgment. **To give us a chance to repent, God has patiently postponed his wrath (2Pe 3:9)**. *But you must remember, while you cannot be sure of the exact time, that day is a certainty. The call to repentance is the reason Jesus came to Earth.*

Rather than spending time with those that considered themselves righteous, Jesus sought out sinners in need of repentance (Lk 5:31-32). *In a similar sense, you should pray for God to increase your sensitivity to your own sinfulness. Your repentance will bring you safely closer to him.*

Like Scrooge, has an awareness of judgment day prodded you to repentance? Give an example.

_____

_____

_____

_____

27

Bob was so forgiving, his wife almost repented of her unforgiveness.
Similarly, you should model forgiveness so that others may repent in humility.
In doing so, you can serve as a living illustration of Christ's law
of forgiveness: having repented of your wrongs and been forgiven,
you pass on forgiveness to those that have wronged you and hopefully
see their repentance in turn (Mt 6:12).

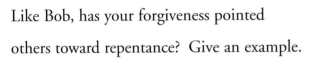

Like Bob, has your forgiveness pointed
others toward repentance? Give an example.

Matthew 6:12
Forgive us our debts, as
we also have forgiven
our debtors.

_____

_____

_____

Like Scrooge, has the example of another
brought you to repentance? Give an example.

_____

_____

_____

Jeremiah 15:19
Therefore this is what
the Lord says: "If you
repent, I will restore
you that you may
serve me; if
you utter worthy, not
worthless, words, you
will be my spokesman.
Let this people turn to
you, but you must not
turn to them."

Scrooge repented of hurting others so he could help them. Likewise,
*God is pleased when our love of others causes us to repent. **If you repent***
of your hateful ways, he will restore you so that you can serve him.
The Lord wants individuals who will be an influence on others for
good (Jer 15:19). *God is waiting for you to turn to him so you can stop*
tearing others down and start building them up.

Like Scrooge, has the desire to improve the lives
of others stirred you to repentance? Give an example.

**The Ghost's line
"If these shadows
remain unaltered
by the Future" is
not in the original
manuscript. It
was a last minute
addition by Dickens,
apparently to give
the reader some
hope for Tiny Tim.**

_____

_____

_____

Action
God Bless Us Every One...

Acts 2:38
Peter replied, "Repent and be baptized, every one of you, in the name of Jesus Christ for the forgiveness of your sins..."

Romans 2:4
Or do you show contempt for the riches of his kindness, tolerance and patience, not realizing that God's kindness leads you toward repentance!

1 JOHN 1: 9-10
If we confess our sins, he is faithful and just and will forgive us our sins and purify us from all unrighteousness. If we claim we have not sinned, we make him out to be a liar and his word has no place in our lives. (NIV)

God welcomes your repentance. In fact, he sent Christ to die so that you could repent. **When you come to Christ, you are forgiven of all of your sins, whether in the past or the present (Acts 2:38).** *Why continue to repent then? When you repent, you show God that you know you have sinned, you confess your sins to him rather than concealing them and you acknowledge you need his power to overcome sin.* **In short, you should continue to repent of your sins so that you can maintain the right relationship with God (Ro 2:4).** *Of course, real repentance involves an attempt to not sin again. In this, you should pray for strength to make good on your repentance.*

Why should you repent?

_____

_____

_____

_____

_____

In one *Carol* play, a real meal was served at the Cratchits. The actress playing Tiny Tim was feeding her poor family with bits of the dinner. Hearing this, Dickens said, "You ought to have given her the whole goose."

How should you repent?

_____

_____

_____

_____

How will God respond
to your repentance?

_____

_____

_____

_____

_____

_____

_____

I will practice repentance in my life by:

❏ Asking for forgiveness from the last person I wronged.

❏ Being ever mindful of the day of judgment.

Specific: _____

_____

_____

According to one critic, "The Ghosts of Christmas Past, Present and Yet To Come are the new Wise Men. And just as these [biblical] kings were led to a poor abode, Scrooge makes a pilgrimage to the humble home of Tiny Tim."

THE STORY

This section, *"Ghost of Christmas Future,"* leads Scrooge
toward salvation, even as he witnesses not one but two deaths.
While the first death is of an unloved man, the second death is
of an angelic child. And while Scrooge is saddened to see the
demise of Tiny Tim, he is distraught to be the death that no one
mourns because of the life he never fully lived. Thus, after facing
his death, he is re-born into a new life—and everyone stands in
awe at the salvation of Scrooge.

THE MORAL OF THE STORY

*This lesson, "The Salvation of Scrooge," highlights the
Biblical principle of Salvation. The study concentrates on how
fortunate we are it is not God's plan for us to suffer but to be
saved—especially since we cannot save ourselves. The notes
also point out that, unfortunately, it often takes a moment
of despair for us to recognize our need for salvation. In
summary, this lesson shows that no amount of work can earn
it—like some material thing—rather our belief in Christ
is our salvation.*

CHARLES DICKENS' *A Christmas Carol Bible Study*

lesson 4

SECTION TITLE: **"Ghost of Christmas Future"**

LESSON TITLE: **"The Salvation of Scrooge"**

BIBLICAL THEME: **Salvation**

LESSON FOUR
"The Salvation of Scrooge"

Unit Overview

Parable

The Christ of Christmas...

1 THESSALONIANS 5:9
For God did not appoint us to suffer wrath but to receive salvation through our Lord Jesus Christ. (NIV)

Reflection

From Humbug to Humble...

2 CORINTHIANS 6:2
For he says, "In the time of my favor I heard you, and in the day of salvation I helped you." I tell you, now is the time of God's favor, now is the day of salvation. (NIV)

Action

God Bless Us Every One...

ACTS 16:30-31
He then brought them out and asked, "Sirs, what must I do to be saved?" They replied, "Believe in the Lord Jesus, and you will be saved—you and your household." (NIV)

Salvation

> **1 THESSALONIANS 5:9**
>
> ***For God did not appoint us to suffer wrath but to receive salvation through our Lord Jesus Christ.*** *(NIV)*

We like salvation so much we look for it everywhere. But it can't be found in our money, our knowledge or our power. Because we cannot save ourselves, we are truly fortunate that it is not God's plan for us to suffer but to be saved. To accomplish this, our Lord Jesus Christ came to offer salvation to all people—through him alone. In other words, Christ did not come to simply encourage us to become better people. Neither did he come to help us save ourselves. Rather, he came to save us from death by sin through the salvation that leads to eternal life.

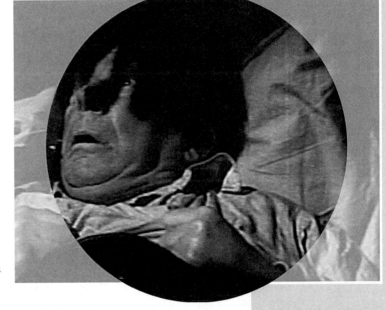

Parable

The Christ of Christmas…

Scrooge faced the darkness of damnation before he saw the light of salvation. To a doomed man like Scrooge, the Ghost of Christmas Future seemed an Angel of Death. And indeed, the Ghost showed him two deaths—one blackened by hatred, the other illuminated by grace. Realizing that he was the hated man, Scrooge plummeted into despair—only to suddenly awaken to a new day and a new life on Christmas morning. Briefly, describe how each responded to salvation.

Scrooge: _____

Ghost: _____

Fred: _____

Bob: _____

Speaking of the death of Scrooge, one character said, "Old Nick has got his own at last, hey?"—"Old Nick" being another name for the Devil.

Do you know that you are saved? If so, what prompted you to accept salvation?

_____

_____

_____

_____

_____

1 Timothy 1:15
Here is a trustworthy saying that deserves full acceptance: Christ Jesus came into the world to save sinners—of whom I am the worst.

Salvation is for sinners. For us, this means if we do not admit we are sinners, we cannot be saved. Indeed, we become more aware of our own sinfulness as we understand more of our salvation through the grace of God. ***Luckily for us, even the worst sinner is not beyond first repenting and then receiving his salvation (1 Ti 1:15).*** *Consider how Scrooge sought salvation.*

How was Scrooge seeking salvation in this visit?
How had his repentance led him to seek salvation?

_____

_____

_____

John 3:17-18
"For God did not send his Son into the world to condemn the world, but to save the world through him. 18) Whoever believes in him is not condemned, but whoever does not believe stands condemned already…"

Salvation can even save a wasted life. Such a life is usually spent in putting faith in the wrong things, like our talents or possessions. ***Although the just reward for this kind of life is eternal death, while we are still here on Earth, it is never too late to turn to Christ for salvation (Jn 3:17-18).*** *The first step is to believe in him— not us. Think about how Scrooge was spurred to salvation.*

Tragically, when he was a boy, Dickens suffered the deaths of both a brother and a sister—which may have been on his mind when writing of the death of Tiny Tim.

What did Scrooge fear more: his death
or his wasted life? How did his death
drive him to save his life?

_____

_____

_____

_____

_____

Why did Scrooge's death point to condemnation?
Why did Tiny Tim's death point to grace?

_____

_____

_____

*Salvation lives. Through the Holy Spirit, which we receive when we
accept the salvation of Christ, Christians gain the power to resist
ungodliness. In this state, we do not have to give in to the temptations
of sin. However, just as important as what we should not do, is what we
should do. **Salvation lives in us when we actively live for God,
loving others as he loves us (Titus 2:11-12).***

How did Scrooge live out his salvation?
How did his actions show he had changed?

_____

_____

_____

Titus 2:11-12
For the grace of God
that brings salvation
has appeared to all
men. 12) It teaches
us to say "No" to
ungodliness and
worldly passions, and
to live self-controlled,
upright and godly lives
in this present age,

Speaking of Tiny Tim,
one reviewer said,
"Through the grace
of the Ghost of
Christmas Present,
Scrooge finds
salvation in this
Christ child-like boy."

Reflection
From Humbug to Humble...

> 2 CORINTHIANS 6:2
> **For he says, "In the time of my favor I heard you, and in the day of salvation I helped you." I tell you, now is the time of God's favor, now is the day of salvation.** *(NIV)*

Salvation is now. While we may wonder about the timing of judgment day, we are saved the moment we accept Christ into our lives and receive God's forgiveness for our sins. Although many people object to the idea that salvation comes through Christ alone, that is the plain teaching of the Bible. **God designated Christ as the only name under heaven that can save you (Ac 4:12).** *Certainly you cannot save yourself from the consequences of your own sins. Unfortunately, it often takes a moment of despair for you to recognize your own insufficiency.* **Following your desires leads to slavery to them (Titus 3:3-5).** *Following Christ leads to eternal freedom.*

Like Scrooge, has a dark moment motivated you to embrace salvation? Give an example.

_____

_____

_____

In the *Carol* book, Dickens wrote of Christmas and Christ, "It is good to be children sometimes, and never better than at Christmas, when its mighty Founder was a child himself."

Bob glimpsed salvation when he saw grace in the death of Tiny Tim. This is the great promise of Christianity—that death is not the end but the beginning of a new life with God. **Just as the Holy Spirit guarantees your redemption, he also gives you the faith you need to take heart at the passing of others, to see grace in the very face of death (Eph 1:13-14).**

Like Bob, have you taken comfort in salvation

at the passing of a loved one? Give an example.

_____

_____

The new Scrooge lived like he was saved. The vision to see beyond the rewards of this world to the salvation in the next gives us tremendous freedom. **Truly, there is no comparison between a temporary prize like money and the everlasting privilege of eternal life—which is particularly shocking when you realize how your love of money can jeopardize your treasure in heaven (Lk 18:22).**
Seek Christ, get saved and give to others.

Like Scrooge, have you lived like

you were saved? Give an example.

_____

_____

_____

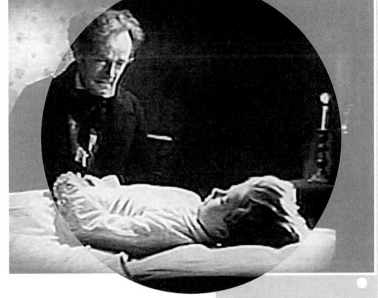

Like Bob, have you been blessed by the

salvation of another? Give an example.

_____

_____

_____

Ephesians 1:13-14
And you also were included in Christ when you heard the word of truth, the gospel of your salvation…you were marked in him with a seal, the promised Holy Spirit, 14) …guaranteeing our inheritance until the redemption…

Luke 18:22
When Jesus heard this, he said to him, "You still lack one thing. Sell everything you have and give to the poor, and you will have treasure in heaven. Then come, follow me."

One lesson that Scrooge must follow in his new life is to be as Christ in the treatment of children—as Scrooge does with Tiny Tim.

Action

God Bless Us Every One...

> ACTS 16:30-31
>
> *He then brought them out and asked, "Sirs, what must I do to be saved?" They replied, "Believe in the Lord Jesus, and you will be saved—you and your household."* (NIV)

Luke 18:25
"Indeed, it is easier for a camel to go through the eye of a needle than for a rich man to enter the Kingdom of God."

Isaiah 59:1-2
Surely the arm of the LORD is not too short to save, nor his ear too dull to hear. 2) But your iniquities have separated you from your God; your sins have hidden his face from you, so that he will not hear.

*What must you do to be saved? Believe in the Lord Jesus. In this way, salvation is offered to all people. You do not receive salvation because you work for it—the way so many material things are received— rather you receive salvation as God's gift. **Nevertheless, in the pursuit of worldly comfort, many delay coming to Christ— and in doing so, some miss their chance entirely (Lk 18:25).** People that are well-off in the world sometimes fail to see that they cannot save themselves in the end. **While sin separates you from God now, unrepentant people who die separate themselves from God for eternity (Isa 59:1-2).** If you are not saved, nothing should keep you from accepting salvation through Christ immediately. If you are saved, live like it—and thereby lead others to salvation in Christ.*

Why can't you save yourself?

_____

_____

_____

_____

At the time of his death, Dickens was so closely linked to the celebration of Christmas that one young girl was reported to have said, "Dickens dead? Then will Father Christmas die too?"

39

How does God save you?

_____

_____

_____

_____

_____

_____

_____

What should you do to be saved?

_____

_____

_____

I will point people toward salvation by:

☐ Living like I am saved, with peace, happiness and love for others.

☐ Telling them how to be saved through Christ—and no other way.

Specific: _____

_____

_____

_____

"I have always striven in my writings to express the veneration for the life and lessons of our Savior..."
Charles Dickens

DEDICATION:
Father
Son
Holy Spirit